Image

Deal with it

from the inside out

Kat Mototsune • Illustrated by Ben Shannon

James Lorimer & Company Ltd., Publishers
Toronto

It's your first day at a new school. And it's like a different planet.

**A**t your old school, you knew exactly who you were and where you belonged. These kids are looking at you like you're an alien.

Who will you sit with?

Over there are some kids in black, with heavy makeup and tattoos. Huddled over a tablet are the tech geeks. The athletes are hanging with the popular kids (what else is new?) and retweeting the latest gossip.

You don't fit in.

No matter where you go, people form groups. The easiest way to ID those groups is by looking at them. But making assumptions about someone because of how they look or who they hang out with can cause all kinds of problems. It can lead to misunderstandings and big-time conflict.

And what about those people who buy into their own image? The ones who spend all their time trying to keep up appearances and go with the crowd. Isn't it sad when the way someone looks on the outside starts to take over the real person underneath?

Want to feel more comfortable with your own image and everyone else's? Read on to learn how you can start feeling more confident in your own skin.

Contents

What is

You know what image is, don't you?

Image is how we appear to others. We have control over some parts of our image, but not over others. Which of the following would you say is a matter of choice?

- your clothes
- how you wear your hair
- the people you spend time with
- how you talk
- the music you listen to
- what you spend your money on
- the celebrities you copy
- your ethnic or racial background
- your age
- your body type
- your reputation

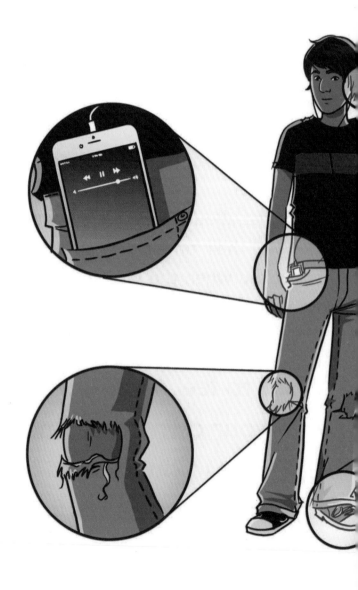

Image?

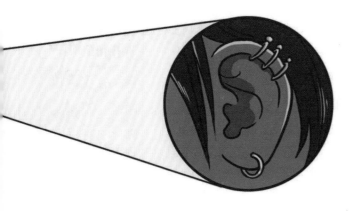

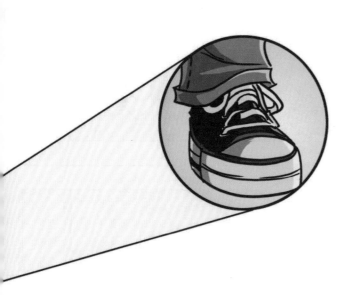

Often, we use these signals about image to sort people into groups. Whatever you call them, it seems like almost every school has:

- jocks
- emos
- goths
- punks
- geeks
- skaters
- tree huggers or hippies
- b-boys and b-girls
- stoners
- indie kids
- hipsters
- preps
- gangstas

… and many more.

It's easy to label someone at a glance. But sometimes what you see is not what you get — and that's how conflicts begin.

Image **101**

People may use image as

a reason to ...

QUIZ

Check the Label

Just like the coolest stuff, image can be all about the label: some things are in and some are out. Sometimes we use labels to include people — to make them feel like they belong. Other times we use them to exclude people — to keep them at a distance. Read the following scenarios and decide if each is an example of **including** or **excluding**. Check your answers on the opposite page.

3 Once the principal finds out that a student has been given detention, he calls them a troublemaker from that point onward.

4 Karen's friends call her "Cure girl" and tease her about listening to old music from the 1980s.

1 Kids tease Leann, calling her the "cootie queen." No one will sit or stand next to her.

5 The rich kids pick on kids who have less, calling them "trailer trash."

2 Jenna and her friends use code names for each other in case people overhear them talking about private things.

6 There's a group of kids that love to crack jokes during class. After their teacher calls them "the Comedians," they decide to perform at the school talent competition.

9 Ella is uncomfortable around some girls who are obsessed with clothes. They call themselves the "style mafia" and stick together.

7 Jamie and his pals get great marks in school. They used to get mad when other kids made fun of their straight A's. Now they laugh it off and call themselves "the A-Team."

10 Will is an amazing rapper. His Black friends call him "White Streak" because he can rap super-fast and come up with great lyrics on the spot.

8 Karen used to be friends with William, but now she hangs with the emos. He calls her a "death head" behind her back.

Answers

1. Excluding
2. Including
3. Excluding
4. Excluding
5. Excluding
6. Including
7. Including
8. Excluding
9. Excluding
10. Including

Dear Conflict Counsellor

Q. **Lately my brother Geordie has started hanging out with a tough gang. He told me they all carry weapons and asked what kind I think he should get. He says it's not like he'd ever really use it. What should I tell him?**

— *Gangsta G's Bro*

A. Geordie's new friends have figured out how to use their image to intimidate people. But does he know the tough look worn by a lot of gang members was inspired by real crime? For example:

*   wearing pants low suggests a person has done jail time (belts are taken from prisoners)
*   huge pants are useful in concealing weapons
*   hoodies are great for making people hard to identify as they run from a crime

Hey, maybe your brother doesn't mind looking like a criminal. Maybe the look is a big part of why he likes being around that gang. In any case, if Geordie hasn't broken the law yet, carrying a weapon will definitely put him over that line. Be a friend to your brother and let him know how that gangsta image could get him into trouble.

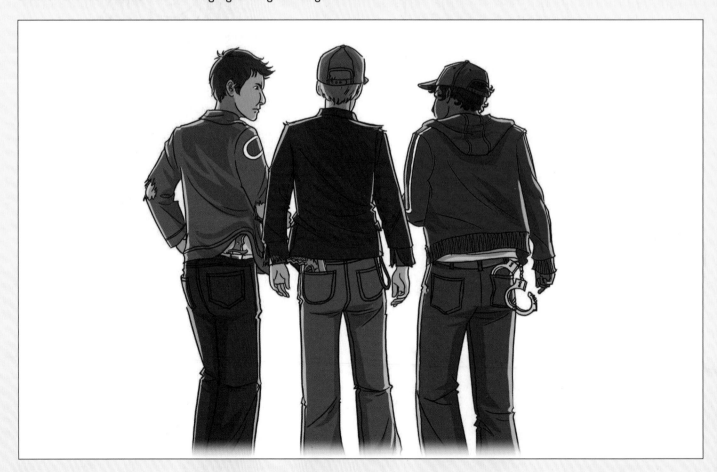

Q. For the first time, I'm part of the popular crowd. It's a lot of work! I have to make sure I have all the right clothes and stuff and keep up my new image even when I'm just hanging out. The worst part is that now my old friends hate me. What should I do?

— *Exhausted Ex-loser*

A. Looks like keeping up a cool image is a lot of work for you. Strange to say, but being popular isn't the same as being liked by everyone. It's just another label. The fact that keeping up appearances takes so much work suggests that your new image doesn't come very naturally to you. You have to decide whether being popular is worth all this stress and energy. And ask yourself this: is hanging with the cool kids (I notice you don't call them friends) worth giving up those who stood by the real you for so long? Think about it.

Q. I love hip-hop music, but I get really mad when I see videos with girls wearing next to nothing and squirming all over the rappers, who are almost always guys.

— *No Ho*

A. You're a good example of how your taste in music doesn't determine everything you are. Don't let those video images limit you. You're too smart to represent yourself as someone who is all looks and no brains. You can find great role models in female hip-hop artists who are strong, talented, and successful in their own right.

Q. I'm one of the few Chinese students at my school. Other kids are always surprised to find out that I'm bad at math, good at basketball, and love country music. Why does my image have to be all about the colour of my skin?

— *Colour Me Average*

A. Those assumptions about your interests are based on a stereotype — a pre-set idea about a group of people. If your friends are just kidding, you can let them know the jokes make you uncomfortable. If they are truly surprised, then you might want to have a more serious conversation. Some people don't realize that so-called positive stereotypes, like being good at math, are as unfair as the negative ones.

Q. Okay, I'm overweight but in good health and pretty cool, too! So why can't I buy clothes that reflect that? The stuff that fits me is frumpy or makes me disappear into the background.

— *No Weighty Wallflower*

A. It's great that you're such a strong, confident person and sad that there aren't more clothes to suit your body and your spirit. Fortunately, designers are starting to clue into the fact that bigger can be beautiful. In the meantime, look for fun shoes and other accessories that reflect your personality. And when you find a great brand, spread the word! Money talks and the fashion industry listens.

Myths

If it walks and talks like a duck, it must be a duck.

If it really wanted to, even a duck could probably change the way it looks and sounds. Don't make quick judgments based on first impressions.

Image is everything.

Like a kitten that thinks its reflection in a mirror is another feline, a person who only sees what's in front of them is bound to end up looking silly.

What you see is what you get.

It's great to represent yourself exactly as you are, but are you sure that everyone is doing the same? Sometimes it's a nice surprise to get even more than you expect!

DID YOU KNOW?

• Social media and online games are all about making friends: 57% of American teens have met a new friend online.

Birds of a feather flock together.

Another bird myth! It's natural to feel more comfortable when you are part of a group. But remember that, even in a flock, every bird is an individual.

It's the package, not the contents.

No matter how important you think the wrapping is, the package doesn't mean a thing without something great inside.

Fitting in is the most important thing.

Fitting in is important to a lot of people, but even more important is finding a group where you can be yourself — even if that means a group of just one.

If I look perfect everyone will like me.

Time to face up to two truths: no one is perfect, and it is impossible for anyone to be liked by everyone.

- These friendships usually stay digital. Only 20% of teens have met an online friend irl.

- For boys, being good at sports is a big part of being popular; for girls, being a social leader is important.

Mirror, mirror on the wall, who has the coolest image of all?

That would be you! You know exactly how to pull yourself together, and you can tell all you need to know about someone at a glance. (Socks plus sandals equals geek, right?) What you see on TV and in magazines helps you build the image you want, and you work hard at it. Is it your fault if other people can't play the game?

Q: I used to be a geek. Not anymore! Over the summer, I got into sports and I'm paying more attention to the clothes I wear. I'm determined to keep improving my image so I can get attention from girls. I have a list of things that I want to buy as soon as I can afford them, like body sprays, sneakers, and exercise equipment. Is there anything else I can do?

— *Project De-Geek*

A: Dr. Shrink-Wrapped thinks that advertisers have done a good job of convincing you that you need the right stuff in order to get attention. Have you ever tried:

- being friendlier?
- becoming a good conversationalist?
- joining clubs with girls who share your interests?
- taking on important issues?
- learning a few jokes?

Dr. Shrink-Wrapped isn't kidding about that last suggestion. Did you know that most girls and women find a good sense of humour to be as attractive as good looks? If you really want to improve your image, start thinking about making changes on the inside.

Q: I usually hang out with the cool kids. Now I have to work on a school project with a girl who's a real loser. She obviously doesn't care what other people think, and all my friends make fun of her. I mean, she's nice and everything, but it's really embarrassing to be around her sometimes. How can I convince my teacher to let me switch partners without hurting this girl's feelings?

— *Afraid to Lose My Cool*

A: Listen, Afraid, it's not like being unpopular is a contagious disease! Dr. Shrink-Wrapped thinks that, under your perfect appearance, you must be pretty insecure about who you really are. If just being seen with someone who's unpopular is enough to destroy your friendships, they can't be great friends. But more likely you just need to learn how to keep your cool when people are making jokes. It's always easier to say than to do, but don't let concerns about your image get in the way of what's really important. Focus on doing well on your project and treat your partner with the same kindness you'd expect if the tables were turned.

QUIZ

Are you the Image-inator?

Do you control your image, or do you let your image control you? Take this quiz to see what you can find out. Of the following statements, how many are true, and how many false?

1 I can tell what people are like just by looking at them.

2 I spend most of my money on the coolest stuff.

3 I don't like being around people who are not like me.

4 I'm a different person at home than I am at school.

5 I have thousands of followers and friends on social media.

6 I tease people if they look strange.

7 Reading blogs, watching TV, and social media show me how I want to look and act.

8 Like it or not, you really need to have the right stuff to be popular.

9 You can judge a book by its cover.

10 Fitting in is important.

11 I like having the power to influence how people feel.

I have nothing to learn from people who are different from me. ⬭ 12

My friends are the only interesting thing at school. ⬭ 13

Very few people really matter. ⬭ 14

Everyone falls into a category. ⬭ 15

Being popular is more important than being smart or nice. ⬭ 16

I'll do almost anything to make people like me. ⬭ 17

I go along when my friends make fun of other people. ⬭ 18

My friends are all like me. ⬭ 19

There are a lot of geeks and losers at my school. ⬭ 20

I spend a lot of time choosing what to wear every day. ⬭ 21

I belong to a gang. ⬭ 22

I hang out with a clique. ⬭ 23

I'd rather die than be fat, ugly, or unfashionable. ⬭ 24

I have to hide what I'm really like inside. ⬭ 25

Did you score a lot of trues? Maybe it's time to realize that real character is more than skin-deep. You might want to talk to someone about how your attitude about image is causing conflicts in your life.

The **Cool Kid**

So fitting in means
everything, right?

There's nothing wrong with loving fashion and style or wanting to feel like you belong. But who decides what's in and what's out? Before you follow a trend, ask yourself a few questions.

What's the message?
Social media, TV, movies, magazines, books, websites, and computer games are full of messages about who you should be and what you should want. Whether or not they are actually ads, these messages are all trying to sell the idea that there could be a "better" you.

What's in It for Them?
Advertisers spend millions and millions of dollars trying to convince you that you need what they are selling. What better way to do that than to keep redefining cool? By constantly starting new trends, companies ensure you keep spending your hard-earned money on more stuff.

Who's Getting Hurt?
Does feeling good about yourself depend on others feeling bad about themselves? Do you throw something away as soon as it becomes popular? Landfills are full of old gadgets, clothes, and toys that people thought they couldn't live without — until everyone else had them too.

Who Are You, Really?
How reasonable is it for everyone to try to look like the same celebrities? Remember that famous people make truckloads of money endorsing products and wearing designer clothes out in public. Instead, how about taking inspiration from risk-takers who have their own unique style?

DID YOU KNOW?

- Kids who are considered cool at 13 tend to be impressed by good-looks and engage in sexual activity earlier than other kids.

do's and don'ts

✓ Do realize that everyone is different.

✓ Do try to make friends outside your own group.

✓ Do make up your own mind about what is important.

✓ Do look beyond someone's image to the real person underneath.

✓ Do challenge your friends if they are treating others badly.

✓ Do explore your own interests.

✓ Do treat everyone with respect.

✗ Don't make snap judgments about people.

✗ Don't confuse image with substance.

✗ Don't expect everyone to want to be just like you.

✗ Don't let the media tell you what you want to be.

✗ Don't let advertisers tell you what you need to have.

✗ Don't admire people for their appearance alone.

✗ Don't treat others badly because of how they look.

✗ Don't label people based on the image they project.

What's the Cost?
Before you buy something, take some time to consider whether it's worth the price. Will you wear or use it many times? Do you own anything like it already? Is there a similar but less expensive option out there? Is it worth more to be like everyone else than to spend money on something important to you? Put the item on hold for a day or two while you make up your mind. You may be surprised by how often you decide to let it go.

- But they are more likely to become alcoholics, addicts and criminals. By the time they are 22, other people their age rate them as less competent.

- Cliques can be based on stereotypes and perceived behaviours. They contribute to your sense of identity and where you think you belong.

They call you a loser.

If they notice you at all. Everyone seems to look right through you. Or they lump you in with kids you have nothing in common with. People say what's inside is all that counts, but sometimes you think you need a better shell.

do's and don'ts

✓ Do avoid kids who set off conflicts.

✓ Do whatever you can to keep your self-esteem.

✓ Do treat other kids as individuals, not as members of groups.

✓ Do remain true to your own values and interests.

✗ Don't break the rules — or the law — to get approval.

✗ Don't spend all your money on stuff just to fit in.

✓ Do respect yourself.

✓ Do remember that other people's values are different from yours.

✓ Do be realistic about your goals for self-improvement.

✗ Don't be ashamed to admit you don't understand or agree with another person's opinion.

✗ Don't let other people decide what should be important to you.

✗ Don't be afraid to talk to someone if the way others treat you becomes unbearable.

QUIZ

Makeover or fake out?

A makeover can be a fun project when you have a realistic goal, like becoming fit and healthy. But sometimes makeovers are motivated by the wrong reasons, like wanting to become someone entirely new. Are you thinking about making a drastic change to your image? Take this quiz, then check your answers on the opposite page to see if your makeover is about making improvements or pretending to be someone you're not.

1 NOT A LITTLE BOY
You look younger than the other guys in your class and hate how people treat you like a little kid. Do you: A) Start lifting weights and talking in a deep voice? B) Act like the mature person you are and take it easy when people guess your age incorrectly?

2 CRUSHABLE
There's a guy at school that you like — he's so nice! — but he's always surrounded by the popular kids. Do you: A) Dress like the other girls and wait for him to notice you? B) Decide a nice person could be attracted to another nice person and look for an opportunity to say hello?

3 LONELY GIRL
Your best friend has transferred to another school, and you're tired of spending every day by yourself. Do you: A) Pick a group to hang out with and clone yourself after them? B) Look into clubs and activities that interest you, and you might make new friends?

4 CLOTHES MAKE THE MAN
You can't afford to dress like the guys you want to hang with. Do you: A) Nag your parents for clothes money? B) Buy only the clothes you really like and can afford and look for other things you have in common with those guys?

22

6 ACE FACE

The results of the first test of the school year came back. You aced it, and now everyone thinks you're a geek. Do you: A) Fail the next test on purpose? B) Find friends to study with who don't resent your higher marks?

7 Junk Jewellery

You bought a bracelet that looks almost like a designer brand. Now some girls are calling you a fake. Do you: A) Beg, borrow, or steal the money to get the real thing? B) Decide that sometimes fake is just fine!

8 Teen Terror

Your family is Muslim and you cover your hair when you go out. Everybody assumes you must be super-religious and secretly hate North Americans. Neither is true. Do you: A) Stop covering your hair when your parents are out of sight? B) Correct people when you have the chance and be proud of who you are?

9 Go Figure

You have developed earlier than most of the other girls. Boys are always staring at your chest. Do you: A) Start wearing a sports bra that hides your curves? B) Concentrate on friendships with boys who treat you with respect?

5 Queer Eye

Rumours have started that you are a lesbian, just because your clothes aren't "girly." Do you: A) Ask your sister to take you shopping? B) Ignore the rumours? Hey, there are worse things than people thinking you're gay and you like to be comfortable!

Answers

If you answered mostly A, you are quick to change to what others expect you to be. Be careful: the real you is in danger of becoming lost.

If you answered mostly B, you try to do your best in difficult situations. And that's all you can ask of yourself while you strive to keep making changes for the better.

How to get back to basics

Count yourself in. Take some time to figure out what kind of person you are and hope to become as you get older. Having a good image without the substance to back it up will only take you so far in life. Get comfortable enough with yourself to base your image on what counts — the truth!

Do the math. What things do you value most? The least? Be honest with yourself, and don't let other people or the media decide how much effort you're going to put into things that aren't very important to you.

Exercise your understanding. It's sad but true that some kids think putting someone else down makes them look better. Instead of getting angry, maybe you should feel sorry for those people. Some of them might be popular now, but very few bullies have friends

Do you feel like you're a victim of your image? Are you tired of feeling bad about your appearance or reputation? There are basic things you can do to feel more confident about the real you.

Learn to read. No, you don't have to go back to the first grade! Take a close look at your friends and classmates and the way they present themselves. Some appear to be super-cool at first sight, but there may be signs that

they are actually pretty insecure. Others might seem totally out of step with everyone else yet are confident about who they are. In other words, don't assume the coolest people are the happiest.

DID YOU KNOW?

• Advertisers cash in on the fact that kids want to have just the right image:

When body image is involved

Think of the ideal body: the perfect picture of what a guy or a girl should be. From the time we are very young, we play with toys, watch movies, and see pictures in books that tell us what a beautiful woman or a handsome man should look like. And now, those "perfect" bodies are everywhere — TV, magazines, websites, games, videos, and plastered all over social media. How many hot selfies posted does it take before you start to compare yourself to the images you see everywhere, and see yourself coming up short?

Do you think I'm sexy?

The ideal body emphasizes the differences between men and women. Girls dream of looking like Barbie® when they grow up, with large breasts, a tiny waist, and freakishly long legs. Boys want to look like their favourite superheros, with massive muscles and flat "six-pack" abs. These images are impossible for most of us to ever attain. And who's to say that real bodies can't be attractive?

Seeing ourselves

Body image is how you perceive your body. More than 40% of men and more than 50% of women surveyed are dissatisfied with how they look. That means about half the population has a negative body image. Not only are they more likely to suffer from depression and low self-esteem, their health can be at risk from:

- dieting
- over-exercising
- use of steroids
- eating disorders
- cosmetic surgery

Behind the Image

If you think about it, there are a lot of silly ideas out there:

- flat-chested women aren't womanly
- thin, physically weak men aren't manly
- overweight people must be lazy and undisciplined
- people with perfect bodies are happier

Not only do these myths cause people to treat others unfairly, they often make us way too hard on ourselves. Imagine if people took all of the effort and the billions of dollars they spend on diet aids and exercise equipment and used it to do some real good in the world!

---

throughout their lives. They are heading down a hard road and you don't have to follow.

Show and Tell. Once you've figured out who you are, it's time to put it out there. You don't have to change overnight, just take little steps towards finding and showing off the real you. For example, once a week try wearing something just for fun, not because it's trendy. Or challenge yourself to speak up when you or someone else is targeted over image issues. With each success, you'll feel stronger and better able to take the next step.

- They'll pay a celebrity more than $10,000 to tweet about their products.

- They slip ads into text updates on favourite TV shows and stars.

- They disguise ads as online videos and games.

There can be a lot of conflict.

Ever see someone being teased, bullied, or excluded because of the way they look? Ever think that someone has an unfair reputation?

Did you say or do anything? Well, why not?

Inside Out

To some extent, everyone — rich or poor, kid or adult — bases the way they deal with others on image. If you've followed the steps on pages 24–25, you are learning to get beyond image and getting practice at being the real you. But how about helping others do the same?

Right-side Out

Unless your school-kid image is hiding mutant superpowers, you can't force people to change. However, you can inspire your friends and family by making changes yourself. You can also start a conversation about what image means to you and the impact you see it having on people's lives. Once you get a dialogue going, you might be surprised to find that you're not the only one who looks beyond image.

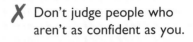

do's and don'ts

✓ Do celebrate the differences between people.

✓ Do support those around you who are being victimized because of their images.

✓ Do respect everyone's right to control their own image.

✓ Do speak up if you disagree with kids you spend time with.

✗ Don't change who you are to achieve a "better" image.

✗ Don't judge people who aren't as confident as you.

✗ Don't make assumptions about people's beliefs.

✗ Don't believe or spread gossip about people based on appearances.

✗ Don't go along with your friends if you disagree with their behaviour.

✗ Don't get involved in "image wars."

✗ Don't let a conflict escalate to violence.

QUIZ

Do you really get it?

It's hard to know what to do when people target others. Sometimes there's no perfect way to react. But you do have choices! What would you do in the following situations? This quiz has no right or wrong answers, because every person is different. Your own solution could be right under the circumstances.

1 IMAGE WARS

Two of the groups at your school are involved in an all-out war. They harass each other in the halls, paint graffiti on lockers, and post awful pictures and stories on their blogs. It's only a matter of time before it will erupt into violence. The principal and teachers are aware of the increased vandalism and fighting, but they don't know that two particular groups are involved.

- Stay away from both groups.
- Leave an anonymous note for the principal.
- Talk to your guidance teacher about how students can help end the conflicts.

2 SECRET FRIENDS

The captain of the school hockey team has asked your best friend out. But he only wants to see her on weekends at places where he won't see anyone from your school. At school, he pretends he doesn't know her.

- Ask your friend why she's with someone who treats her badly.
- Encourage her to spend time with people who value her as a person.
- Support your friend and be there to listen.

3 BIG BUSINESS

You're on the bus when a tough-looking girl gets on. She dresses like one of those kids who clean car windows and then ask for money. Even though she has bus fare, the driver says loudly that he won't have her getting on and harassing his passengers.

- Tell the driver it's unfair to make assumptions about the girl.
- Get off the bus and wait for the girl for the next one.
- Inform the transit company what you witnessed.

4 Pumping Up

Your friend has decided that he needs to build muscle to attract girls. He is spending all his time in the gym or recovering from his extreme workouts, but he still isn't satisfied with the results. Now you know he has managed to get some steroids.

- Tell your friend about the dangers of using steroids.
- Tell him you can't hang out with someone who takes drugs.
- Look for a "clean" bodybuilder who could be a good role model.

5 EXTREME MAKEOVER

Your cousin has started saving all of her money so she can get a nose job some day. She thinks her nose is the reason she doesn't have a boyfriend.

- Tell your cousin all the things you like about her.
- Suggest other ways she could feel more attractive.
- Show her examples of beautiful women with unconventional features.

Continues . . .

6 Vomit Comet

There's a girl at school who everyone thinks is perfect — they all want to be like her. You've walked in on her throwing up in the girls' washroom.

- Find out whether she's sick and needs help.
- Ask if she has a problem she wants to discuss.
- Talk to your guidance teacher about doing a seminar on eating disorders.

7 BRAIN TRUST

Your friend has always gotten great grades, and he is proud of his position as leader of the Brains. But you know that he cheated on his last science test.

- Tell him you know he cheated and disapprove of it.
- Ask your friend if he wants help studying for the next test.
- Leave an anonymous note for the science teacher.

8 Romeo and Juliet

Your brother and his girlfriend belong to two conflicting groups at school. Your brother's friends have approached you about causing trouble between them so that everything can go back to normal.

- Warn your brother about the plan.
- Talk to your brother, telling him what his friends have asked and asking him if he really cares enough about the girl to alienate his friends.
- Support your brother and his girlfriend.

DID YOU KNOW?

- The more you weigh, the more you weigh! Teen girls who step on the scale a lot are more likely to gain weight.

9 WHITE OUT

You know that part of the initiation into the white gang at school involves secretly beating up someone of colour. Now there's a new kid in the gang and it's only a matter of time until someone gets hurt.

- Talk to your parents about going to the police.
- Help coordinate an anti-violence campaign at your school.
- Ensure students who are at risk have been informed of the danger.

10 PAINT IT BLACK

There has been a lot of talk about a rash of teen suicides in a nearby community. You overhear kids in the lunchroom discussing websites that describe ways to kill yourself and following social media posts on forming a suicide club.

- Ask one of the kids in the group how serious they are about suicide.
- Tell the principal what you overheard (anonymously, if necessary).
- Watch for students who seem very depressed and may need help.

- The gang image is so popular, kids will form neighbourhood groups or cliques that look and act like criminal gangs.

- About 5% of youth suicides are influenced by suicide contagion, or exposure to the idea of suicide through the media.

More **Help**

It takes time and practice to learn the skills in this book. There are many ways to manage your image and to deal with conflicts about it, but only you know what feels right for you in different situations. In the end, the best response is the one that lets you be you.

If you need more information or someone to talk to, these resources might help.

Helplines

Kids Help Phone 1-800-668-6868
Youth Crisis Hotline 1-800-448-4663
Teen Line 1-800-TLC-TEEN; text TEEN to 839863

Web sites

Adios, Barbie www.adiosbarbie.com
The Canadian Safe School Network www.canadiansafeschools.com
KidsHealth www.kidshealth.org
Kids Help Phone www.kidshelpphone.ca

Books

A Christmas Kerril by Denise Jaden. Self-published, 2015.
Because of Mr. Terupt by Rob Buyea. Yearling, 2011.
The Gutsy Girl: Escapades for your Life of Epic Adventure by Caroline Paul. Bloomsbury Press, 2016.
Jane, the Fox and Me by Fanny Britt. Groundwood Books, 2013.
Making the Team, by Kelsey Blair. James Lorimer & Co., 2016.
Max the Mighty by Rodman Philbrick. Scholastic, 2013.
Stepping Out by Laura Langston. Orca, 2015.
28 Tricks for a Fearless Grade 6 by Catherine Austen. James Lorimer & Co., 2014.
26 Tips for Surviving Grade 6 by Catherine Austen. James Lorimer & Co., 2014.
Two Strikes by Johnny Boateng. James Lorimer & Co., 2016.
Wonder by R.J. Palacio. Knopf, 2014.

Graphic Novel

Queen Bee by Chynna Clugston. Scholastic, 2005.

Videos

Beef. National Film Board, 2010.
Miss Representation/The Mask You Live In. The Representation Project, 2015.
Staying Real: Teens Confront Sexual Stereotypes. National Film Board, 2010.

Some other titles in the Deal With It series

Girlness: Deal with it body and soul by Diane Peters, illustrated by Steven Murray.
Guyness: Deal with it body and soul by Steve Pitt, illustrated by Steven Murray.
Teasing: Deal with it before the joke's on you by Steve Pitt, illustrated by Remie Geoffroi.
Privacy: Deal with it like nobody's business by Diane Peters, illustrated by Jeremy Tankard.
Gossip: Deal with it before word gets around by Catherine Rondina, illustrated by Dan Workman.
Transphobia: Deal with it and be a gender transcender by j wallace skelton, illustrated by Nick Johnson.

James Lorimer & Company Ltd., Publishers acknowledges the support of the Ontario Arts Council (OAC), an agency of the Government of Ontario. We acknowledge the support of the Canada Council for the Arts, which last year invested $153 million to bring the arts to Canadians throughout the country. This project has been made possible in part by the Government of Canada and with the support of the Ontario Media Development Corporation.

Canada Council   Conseil des Arts
for the Arts   du Canada

Canada

ONTARIO ARTS COUNCIL
CONSEIL DES ARTS DE L'ONTARIO

Series design: Blair Kerrigan/Glyphics
Cover image: Shutterstock

Library and Archives Canada Cataloguing in Publication

Mototsune, Kat, author
       Image : deal with it from the inside out / Kat Mototsune ; illustrated by Ben Shannon. -- [New edition]

(Deal with it)
ISBN 978-1-4594-1188-3 (hardback)

       1. Conformity--Juvenile literature. 2. Peer pressure--Juvenile literature. I. Shannon, Ben, illustrator II. Title. III. Series: Deal with it (Toronto, Ont.)

BF323.S63M68 2017   j303.3'2   C2016-906887-0

James Lorimer & Company Ltd., Publishers
117 Peter Street, Suite 304
Toronto, ON, Canada
M5V 0M3
www.lorimer.ca

American edition published in 2017
Distributed by: Lerner Publishing Group
1251 Washington Ave N
Minneapolis, MN, USA
55401

Printed and bound in Hong Kong.